Special Thank-You to my husband and kids for their encouragement and support. Love ya'll more!

D1319586

And to offer a scrifice according to that which is said in the law of the Lord, A pair of turtledoves, or two young pigeons.

Luke 2:24

Sermon Notes	Date:.................................
	Location:............................
	Speaker:.............................
	Title:...............................

....
....
....
....
....
....
....
....
....
....

Scripture References	....
	....
	....

| **_Prayer Requests:_** | .... |
| | .... |

And when they were come into the house, they
saw the young child with Mary, his mother,
and fell down, and worshipped him: and when
they had opened their treasures, they presented
unto him gifts: gold, frankincense, and myrrh.

Matthew 2:11

Sermon Notes	Date:................................
	Location:...........................
	Speaker:............................
	Title:...............................

....

....

....

....

....

....

....

....

....

....

Scripture References	....
	....
	....
Prayer Requests:	....
	....

And lo a voice from heaven, saying, This is my beloved Son, in whom I am well pleased.

Matthew 3:17

Sermon Notes	Date:.............................
	Location:..........................
	Speaker:...........................
	Title:.............................

....

....

....

....

....

....

....

....

....

....

Scripture References	....
	....
	....
Prayer Requests:	....
	....

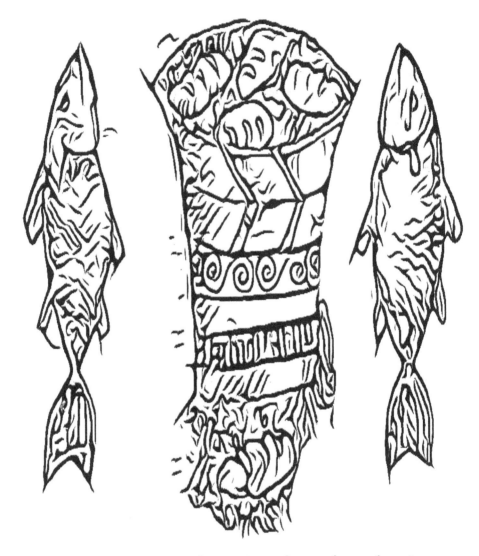

And they say unto him, We have here but five loaves, and two fishes. He said, Bring them hither to me.

Matthew 14:17-18

Sermon Notes

Date:..............................

Location:..........................

Speaker:..........................

Title:..............................

....

....

....

....

....

....

....

....

....

....

Scripture References

....

....

....

Prayer Requests:

....

....

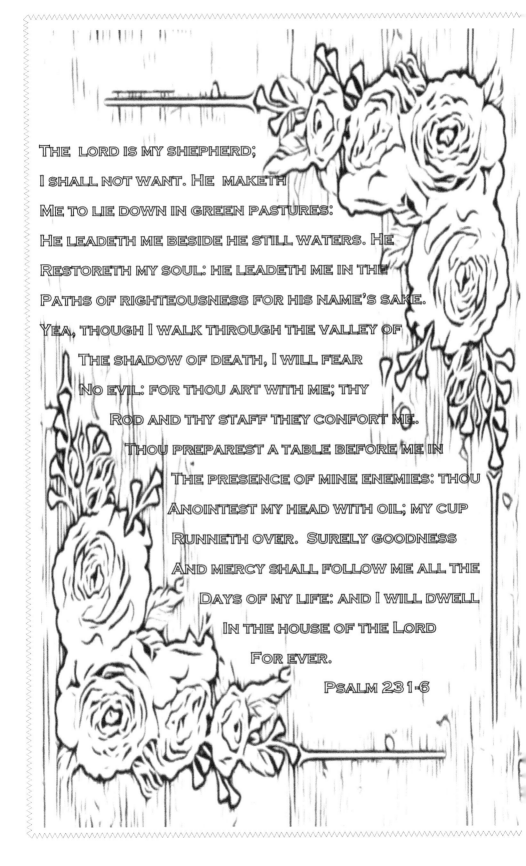

The lord is my shepherd;
I shall not want. He maketh
Me to lie down in green pastures:
He leadeth me beside he still waters. He
Restoreth my soul: he leadeth me in the
Paths of righteousness for his name's sake.
Yea, though I walk through the valley of
The shadow of death, I will fear
No evil: for thou art with me; thy
Rod and thy staff they confort me.
Thou preparest a table before me in
The presence of mine enemies: thou
Anointest my head with oil; my cup
Runneth over. Surely goodness
And mercy shall follow me all the
Days of my life: and I will dwell
In the house of the Lord
For ever.

Psalm 23 1-6

Sermon Notes	Date:..............................
	Location:...........................
	Speaker:...........................
	Title:..............................

....

....

....

....

....

....

....

....

....

....

Scripture References	....
	....
	....
Prayer Requests:	....
	....

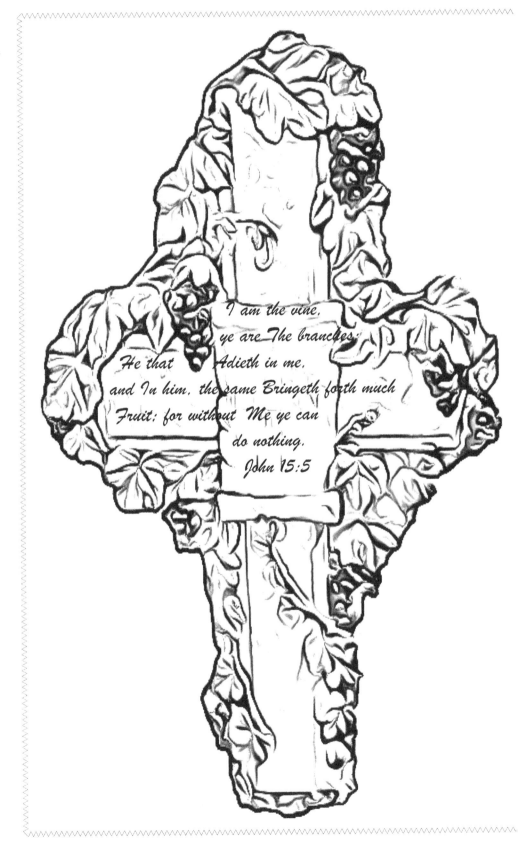

Sermon Notes

Date: ....

Location: ....

Speaker: ....

Title: ....

....
....
....
....
....
....
....
....
....
....

Scripture References

....
....
....

Prayer Requests:

....
....

For God so loved the world, that he gave his only begotten Son, that whosoever believeth in him should not perish, but have everlasting life.

John 3:16

Sermon Notes

Date: ....

Location: ....

Speaker: ....

Title: ....

....

....

....

....

....

....

....

....

....

....

Scripture References

....

....

....

Prayer Requests:

....

....

The thief cometh not, but for to steal, and to
kill, and to destroy: I am come that they might
have life, and that they might have it more
abundantly.

John 10:10

Sermon Notes

Date:................................

Location:............................

Speaker:.............................

Title:...............................

....

....

....

....

....

....

....

....

....

....

Scripture References

....

....

....

Prayer Requests:

....

....

All go unto one place; all are of the dust, and

all turn to dust again.

Ecclesiastes 3:20

Sermon Notes

Date: ....

Location: ....

Speaker: ....

Title: ....

....

....

....

....

....

....

....

....

....

....

Scripture References

....

....

....

Prayer Requests:

....

....

But go ye and learn what that meaneth, I will
have mercy, and not sacrifice: for I am not
come to call the righteous, but sinners to
repentance.

Matthew 9:13

Sermon Notes	Date:...............................
	Location:...........................
	Speaker:...........................
	Title:..............................

....
....
....
....
....
....
....
....
....
....

Scripture References	....
	....
	....
Prayer Requests:	....
	....

The Lord thy God in the midst of thee is
mighty; he will save, he will rejoice over thee
with joy; he will rest in his love, he will joy
over thee with singing.

Zephaniah 3:17

Sermon Notes	Date:........................
	Location:......................
	Speaker:......................
	Title:........................

....
....
....
....
....
....
....
....
....
....

Scripture References	....
	....
	....
Prayer Requests:	....
	....

For they all saw him, and were troubled. And immediately he talked with them, and saith unto them, Be of good cheer: it is I; be not afraid.

Mark 6:50

Sermon Notes

Date: ....

Location: ....

Speaker: ....

Title: ....

....

....

....

....

....

....

....

....

....

....

Scripture References

....

....

....

Prayer Requests:

....

....

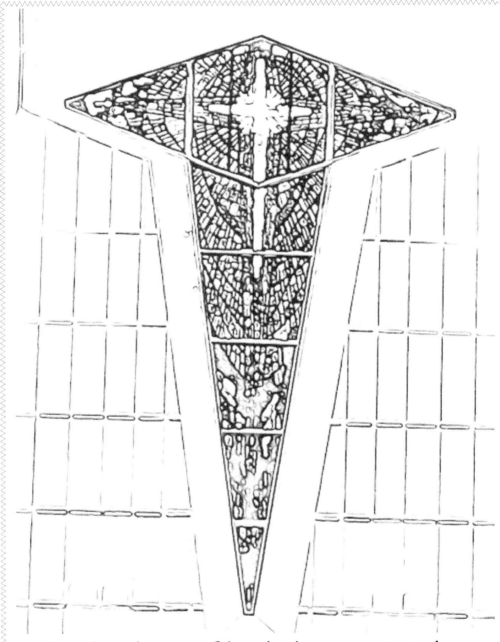

And they that are Christ's have crucified the flesh with the affections and lusts.

Galatians 5:24

Sermon Notes	Date: .... Location: .... Speaker: .... Title: ....

....
....
....
....
....
....
....
....
....
....

Scripture References	....
Prayer Requests:	....

But Jesus called them unto him, and said,
Suffer little children to come unto me, and
forbid them not: for of such is the kingdom of
God.

Luke 18:16

Sermon Notes

Date:...............................

Location:...........................

Speaker:............................

Title:..............................

....

....

....

....

....

....

....

....

....

....

Scripture References

....

....

....

Prayer Requests:

....

....

Took branches of palm trees, and went forth to meet him, and cried, Hosanna: Blessed it the King of Israel that cometh in the name of the Lord.

John 12:13

Sermon Notes

Date:..............................

Location:..........................

Speaker:...........................

Title:.............................

....
....
....
....
....
....
....
....
....
....

Scripture References

....
....
....

Prayer Requests:

....
....

And as they were eating, Jesus took bread, and blessed it, and brake it, and gave it to the disciples, and said, Take, eat; this is my body.

Matthew 26:26

Sermon Notes

Date:.............................

Location:.........................

Speaker:..........................

Title:............................

....

....

....

....

....

....

....

....

....

....

Scripture References

....

....

....

Prayer Requests:

....

....

And when Jesus had cried with a loud voice, he said, Father, into thy hands I commend my spirit: and having said thus, he gave up the ghost.

Luke 23:46

Sermon Notes	Date:............................ Location:......................... Speaker:.......................... Title:............................

....
....
....
....
....
....
....
....
....
....

Scripture References	....
Prayer Requests:	....

He is not here: for he is risen, as he said.

Come, see the place where the Lord lay.

Matthew 28:6

Sermon Notes	Date:...............................
	Location:..........................
	Speaker:...........................
	Title:.............................

....
....
....
....
....
....
....
....
....
....

Scripture References	....
	....
	....
Prayer Requests:	....
	....

Rejoice ye in that day, and leap for joy: for,
behold, your reward is great in heaven: for in
the like manner did their fathers unto the
prophets.

Luke 6:23

Sermon Notes

Date: ....

Location: ....

Speaker: ....

Title: ....

....

....

....

....

....

....

....

....

....

....

Scripture References

....

....

....

Prayer Requests:

....

....

And Jesus said unto them, Because of your
unbelief: for verily I say unto you, If ye have
faith as a grain of mustard seed, ye shall say
unto this mountain, Remove hence to yonder
place; and it shall remove; and nothing shall be
impossible unto you.

Matthew 17:20

Sermon Notes

Date:...............................

Location:..........................

Speaker:...........................

Title:.............................

....

....

....

....

....

....

....

....

....

....

Scripture References

....

....

....

Prayer Requests:

....

....

Verily, verily, I say unto you, That ye shall weep and lament, but the world shall rejoice: and ye shall be sorrowful, but your sorrow shall be turned into joy.

John 16:20

Sermon Notes

Date: ....

Location: ....

Speaker: ....

Title: ....

....

....

....

....

....

....

....

....

....

....

Scripture References

....

....

....

Prayer Requests:

....

....

And ye now therefore have sorrow: but I will
see you again, and your heart shall rejoice,
and your joy no man taketh from you.

John 16:22

Sermon Notes

Date:..............................

Location:..........................

Speaker:..........................

Title:.............................

....

....

....

....

....

....

....

....

....

....

Scripture References

....

....

....

Prayer Requests:

....

....

She is more precious than rubies: and all the things thou canst desire are not to be compared unto her.

Proverbs 3:15

Sermon Notes

Date: ....

Location: ....

Speaker: ....

Title: ....

....

....

....

....

....

....

....

....

....

....

Scripture References

....

....

....

Prayer Requests:

....

....

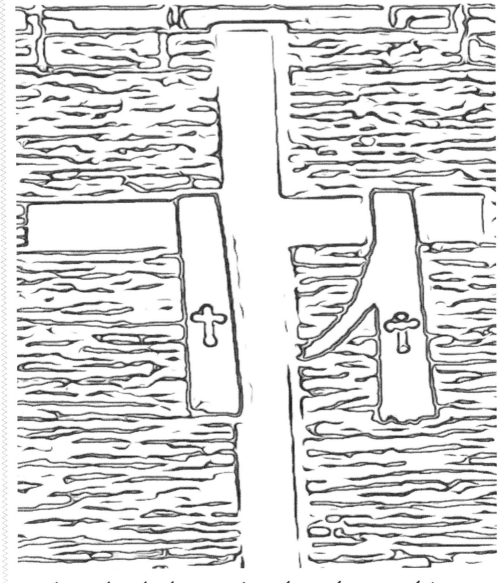

And when he had spoken these things, while
they beheld, he was taken up; and a cloud
received him out of their sight.

Acts 1:9

Sermon Notes	Date:.............................
	Location:.........................
	Speaker:..........................
	Title:............................

....
....
....
....
....
....
....
....
....
....

Scripture References	....
	....
	....

| _Prayer Requests:_ | .... |
| | .... |

And suddenly there came a sound from heaven
as of a rushing mighty wind, and it filled all
the house where they were sitting.

Acts 2:2

Sermon Notes	Date:.............................
	Location:.........................
	Speaker:..........................
	Title:............................

....
....
....
....
....
....
....
....
....
....

Scripture References	....
	....
	....

| *Prayer Requests:* | .... |
| | .... |

The grace of the Lord Jesus Christ, and the love of God, and the communion of the Holy Ghost, be with you all. Amen.

2Corinthians 13:14

Sermon Notes

Date: ....
Location: ....
Speaker: ....
Title: ....

....
....
....
....
....
....
....
....
....
....

Scripture References

....
....
....

Prayer Requests:

....
....

Wherefore take unto you the whole armour of God, that ye may be able to withstand in the evil day, and having done all, to stand.

Ephesians 6:13

Sermon Notes

Date: ....
Location: ....
Speaker: ....
Title: ....

....
....
....
....
....
....
....
....
....
....

Scripture References

....
....
....

Prayer Requests:

....
....

These things I command you, that ye love one another.

John 15:17

Sermon Notes	Date:...............................
	Location:............................
	Speaker:.............................
	Title:...............................

....

....

....

....

....

....

....

....

....

....

Scripture References	....
	....
	....

| _Prayer Requests:_ | .... |
| | .... |

The father of the righteous shall greatly rejoice:
and he that begetteth a wise child shall have joy
of him.

Proverbs 23:24

Sermon Notes	Date: ....
	Location: ....
	Speaker: ....
	Title: ....

....
....
....
....
....
....
....
....
....
....

Scripture References	....
	....
	....

| *Prayer Requests:* | .... |
| | .... |

But they that wait upon the Lord shall renew their strength; they shall mount up with wings as eagles; they shall run, and not be weary, and they shall walk, and not faint.

Isaiah 40:31

Sermon Notes

Date:...............................

Location:..........................

Speaker:..........................

Title:..............................

....

....

....

....

....

....

....

....

....

....

Scripture References

....

....

....

Prayer Requests:

....

....

Every branch in me that beareth not fruit he taketh away: and every branch that beareth fruit, he purgeth it, that it may bring forth more fruit.

John 15:2

Sermon Notes

Date:.............................

Location:..........................

Speaker:..........................

Title:.............................

....

....

....

....

....

....

....

....

....

....

Scripture References

....

....

....

Prayer Requests:

....

....

Abide in me, and I in you. As the branch
cannot bear fruit of itself, except it abide in the
vine; no more can ye, except ye abide in me.

John 15:4

Sermon Notes

Date: ....

Location: ....

Speaker: ....

Title: ....

....

....

....

....

....

....

....

....

....

....

Scripture References

....

....

....

Prayer Requests:

....

....

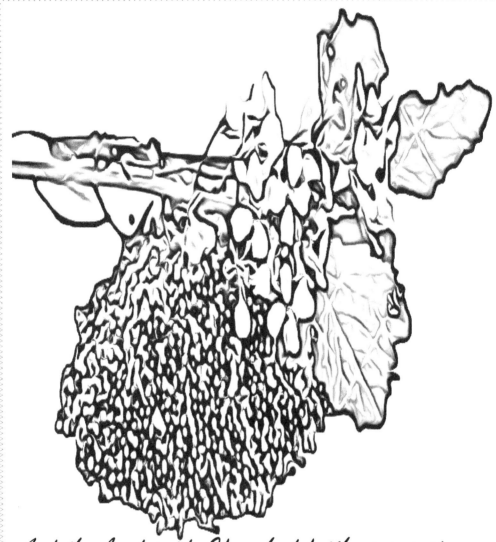

And the Lord said, If ye had faith as a grain of mustard seed, ye might say unto this sycamine tree, Be thou plucked up by the root, and be thou planted in the sea; and it should obey you.

Luke 17:6

Sermon Notes	Date:...............................
	Location:............................
	Speaker:.............................
	Title:...............................

....
....
....
....
....
....
....
....
....
....

| *Scripture References* | ....
....
.... |
| *Prayer Requests:* | ....
.... |

AFTER THIS MANNER THEREFORE PRAY YE: OUR FATHER WHICH ART IN HEAVEN, HALLOWED BE THY NAME. THY KINGDOM COME. THY WILL BE DONE IN EARTH, AS IT IS IN HEAVEN. GIVE US THIS DAY OUR DAILY BREAD. AND FORGIVE US OUR DEBTS, AS WE FORGIVE OUR DEBTORS. AND LEAD US NOT INTO TEMPTATION, BUT DELIVER US FROM EVIL: FOR THINE IS THE KINGDOM, AND THE POWER, AND THE GLORY, FOR EVER. AMEN.

MATTHEW 6:9-13

Sermon Notes

Date: ....

Location: ....

Speaker: ....

Title: ....

....

....

....

....

....

....

....

....

....

....

Scripture References

....

....

....

Prayer Requests:

....

....

But the fruit of the Spirit is love, joy, peace, longsuffering, gentleness, goodness, faith, Meekness, temperance: against such there is no law.

Galatians 5:22-23

Sermon Notes

Date:.................................

Location:.............................

Speaker:.............................

Title:................................

....
....
....
....
....
....
....
....
....
....

Scripture References

....
....
....

Prayer Requests:

....
....

Wherefore laying aside all malice, and all guile, and hypocrisies, and envies, and all evil speakings. As newborn babes, desire the sincere milk of the word, that ye may grow thereby: If so be ye have taste that the Lord is gracious.

1 Peter 2:1-3

Sermon Notes

Date:...............................

Location:..........................

Speaker:...........................

Title:.............................

....

....

....

....

....

....

....

....

....

....

Scripture References

....

....

....

Prayer Requests:

....

....

But ye, beloved, building up yourselves on your most holy faith, praying in the Holy Ghost.

Jude 1:20

Sermon Notes

Date:................................

Location:...........................

Speaker:............................

Title:...............................

....

....

....

....

....

....

....

....

....

....

Scripture References

....

....

....

Prayer Requests:

....

....

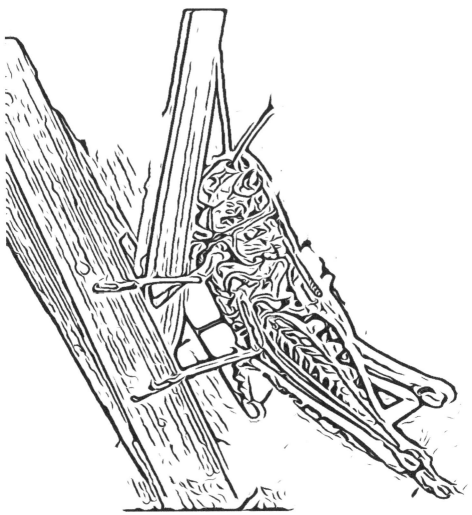

It is he that sitteth upon the circle of the earth,

and the inhabitants thereof are as grasshoppers;

that stretcheth out the heavens as a curtain,

and spreadeth them out as a tent to dwell in:

Isaiah 40:22

Sermon Notes

Date:..............................

Location:..........................

Speaker:...........................

Title:.............................

....

....

....

....

....

....

....

....

....

....

Scripture References

....

....

....

Prayer Requests:

....

....

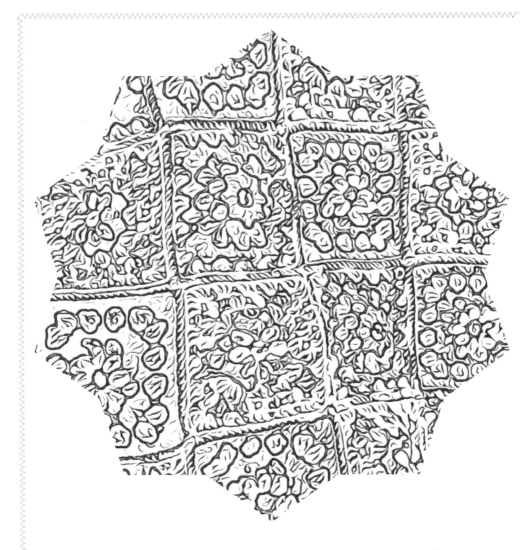

And out of the ground made the Lord God to grow every tree that is pleasant to the sight, and good for food; the tree of life also in the midst of the garden, and the tree of knowledge of good and evil.

Genesis 2:9

Sermon Notes

Date: ....

Location: ....

Speaker: ....

Title: ....

....

....

....

....

....

....

....

....

....

....

Scripture References

....

....

....

Prayer Requests:

....

....

Jesus saith unto them, Fill the waterpots with water. And they filled them up to the brim. And he saith unto them, Draw out now, and bear unto the governor of the feast. And they bare it.

John 2:7-8

Sermon Notes

Date: ....

Location: ....

Speaker: ....

Title: ....

....

....

....

....

....

....

....

....

....

....

Scripture References

....

....

....

Prayer Requests:

....

....

And saith unto him, Every man at the beginning doth set forth good wine; and when men have well drunk, then that which is worse: but thou hast kept the good wine until now.

John 2:10

Sermon Notes	Date:..............................
	Location:..........................
	Speaker:...........................
	Title:.............................

....
....
....
....
....
....
....
....
....
....

Scripture References	....
	....
	....
Prayer Requests:	....
	....

This is the day which the Lord hath made; we will rejoice and be glad in it.

Psalm 118:24

	Date:...............................
**Sermon Notes**	Location:..........................
	Speaker:...........................
	Title:...............................

....

....

....

....

....

....

....

....

....

....

**Scripture References**	....
	....
	....
**Prayer Requests:**	....
	....

I WILL PRAISE THEE; FOR I AM FEARFULLY AND WONDERFULLY MADE: MARVELLOUS ARE THY WORKS; AND THAT MY SOUL KNOWETH RIGHT WELL. PSALM 139:14

Sermon Notes

Date: ....

Location: ....

Speaker: ....

Title: ....

....

....

....

....

....

....

....

....

....

....

Scripture References

....

....

....

Prayer Requests:

....

....

Rejoice evermore. Pray without ceasing. In everything give thanks: for this is the will of God in Christ Jesus concerning you.

1 Thessalonians 5:16-18

Sermon Notes

Date:..............................

Location:..........................

Speaker:...........................

Title:.............................

....

....

....

....

....

....

....

....

....

....

Scripture References

....

....

....

Prayer Requests:

....

....

I can do all things through Christ which strengtheneth me.

Philippians 4:13

Sermon Notes

Date:........................

Location:......................

Speaker:......................

Title:........................

....

....

....

....

....

....

....

....

....

....

Scripture References

....

....

....

Prayer Requests:

....

....

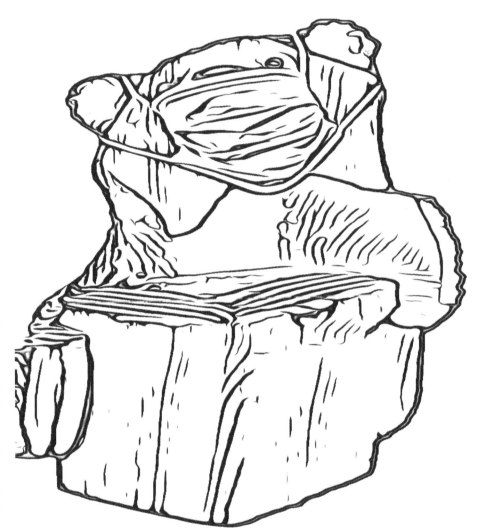

And he answering said, Thou shalt love the
Lord thy God with all thy heart, and with all
thy soul, and with all thy strength, and with
all thy mind; and thy neighbour as thyself.

Luke 10:27

Sermon Notes

Date:................................

Location:..........................

Speaker:...........................

Title:.............................

....

....

....

....

....

....

....

....

....

....

Scripture References

....

....

....

Prayer Requests:

....

....

O give thanks unto the Lord, for he is good:

for his mercy endureth for ever.

Psalm 107:1

Sermon Notes

Date:..............................
Location:..........................
Speaker:..........................
Title:.............................

....
....
....
....
....
....
....
....
....
....

Scripture References

....
....
....

Prayer Requests:

....
....

That if thou shalt confess with thy mouth the Lord Jesus, and shalt believe in thine heart that God hath raised him from the dead, thou shalt be saved.

Romans 10:9

Sermon Notes

Date:..............................

Location:..........................

Speaker:...........................

Title:.............................

....

....

....

....

....

....

....

....

....

....

Scripture References

....

....

....

Prayer Requests:

....

....

Saying, Amen: Blessing, and glory, and wisdom, and thanksgiving, and honour, and power, and might, be unto God for ever and ever. Amen.

Revelation 7:12

Sermon Notes	Date:.................................
	Location:..........................
	Speaker:...........................
	Title:..............................

....
....
....
....
....
....
....
....
....
....

Scripture References	....
	....
	....

| **Prayer Requests:** | .... |
| | .... |

Giving thanks always for all things unto God and the Father in the name of our Lord Jesus Christ.

Ephesians 5:20

Sermon Notes

Date:..............................

Location:..........................

Speaker:...........................

Title:.............................

....

....

....

....

....

....

....

....

....

....

Scripture References

....

....

....

Prayer Requests:

....

....

And at the dedication of the wall of Jerusalem they sought the Levites out of all their places, to bring them to Jerusalem, to keep the dedication with gladness, both with thanksgiving, and with singing, with cymbals, psalteries, and with harps.

Nehemiah 12:27

	Date:............................
Sermon Notes	Location:.........................
	Speaker:.........................
	Title:...........................

....

....

....

....

....

....

....

....

....

....

	....
Scripture References	....
	....
Prayer Requests:	....
	....

Now the God of hope fill you with all joy and peace in believing, that ye may abound in hope, through the power of the Holy Ghost.

Romans 15:13

Sermon Notes

Date: ....

Location: ....

Speaker: ....

Title: ....

....

....

....

....

....

....

....

....

....

....

Scripture References

....

....

....

Prayer Requests:

....

....

Glory to God in the highest, and on earth peace, good will toward men.

Luke 2:14

Sermon Notes

Date:.............................

Location:.........................

Speaker:.........................

Title:............................

....
....
....
....
....
....
....
....
....
....

Scripture References

....
....
....

Prayer Requests:

....
....

And the angel said unto them, Fear not: for behold, I bring you good tidings of great joy, which shall be to all people. For unto you is born this day in the city of David a Saviour, which is Christ the Lord.

Luke 2:10-11

	Date:................................
Sermon Notes	Location:............................
	Speaker:............................
	Title:..............................

....

....

....

....

....

....

....

....

....

....

Scripture References	....
	....
	....
Prayer Requests:	....
	....

And we have known and believed the love that God hath to us. God is love; and he that dwelleth in love dwelleth in God, and God in him.

1 John 4:16

Sermon Notes	Date:............................... Location:........................... Speaker:............................ Title:..............................

....
....
....
....
....
....
....
....
....
....

Scripture References	....
Prayer Requests:	....

And Joseph also went up from Galilee, out of the city of Nazareth, into Judaea, unto the city of David, which is called Bethlehem; (because he was of the house and lineage of David:) To be taxed with Mary his espoused wife, being great with child.

Luke 2:4-5

Sermon Notes

Date:.................................

Location:............................

Speaker:.............................

Title:...............................

....

....

....

....

....

....

....

....

....

....

Scripture References

....

....

....

Prayer Requests:

....

....

And she brought forth her firstborn son. And
wrapped him in swaddling clothes, and laid hm
in a manger, because there was no room for
them in the inn.

Luke 2:7

Sermon Notes	Date:...........................
	Location:.........................
	Speaker:..........................
	Title:............................

....
....
....
....
....
....
....
....
....
....

Scripture References	....
	....
	....
Prayer Requests:	....
	....

Made in the USA
Coppell, TX
03 February 2023

12020584R00066